Muu-So
The Story of Creation

Muu-So: The Story of Creation

by Coumba Toure

illustrations by Rokhaya Gueye

Daraja Press

Published by Daraja Press
www.darajapress.com
First published by Falia Editions Enfance, Dakar, Senegal
Text ©2017 Coumba Touré
Illustrations © Ndeye Rokhaya Gueye
Falia Editions Enfance is a publishing house that seeks to produce for children
and with children based in Dakar - Senegal West Africa
Graphic design: Elie Calhoun/Tidiane Oumar Ba
Editorial support: Tidiane Oumar BA

Library and Archives Canada Cataloguing in Publication

Touré, Coumba, author
          Muu-So : the story of creation / by Coumba Touré ; illustrations
by Rokhaya Gueye.

Issued in print and electronic formats.
ISBN 978-0-9953474-3-4 (softcover).--ISBN 978-0-9953474-4-1 (ebook)

          1. Creation--Mythology--Mali--Juvenile literature. 2. Creation--
Mythology--Senegal--Juvenile literature. I. Gueye, Rokhaya, illustrator
II. Title.

BL325.7.T68 2017   j202'.4   C2017-901039-5

                                                              C2017-901040-9

To Suzanne Fau, my mother,
To Mareme Mbodj, her Mother
To Seynabou Mbengue, her grandmother...
To the first mother ever on earth.

"To
those
willing to
carry the clay
pot called Muu,
I will give the power
of balance and a sense
of justice," declared the
supreme deity Maa
Ngala Ba
at the dawn of
creation.

"They will have the ability
to give birth to new lives,
new minds and new worlds.

They will be named Muu-So,
the pot carriers, and they will
come back to life again and
again in future generations."

Indeed, at the beginning, Maa Ngala Ba first created the wind and stars. She then created the earth and the rain. Afterwards, she created the plants and the animals in the bush.

3

Then, she blew very hard on all of her creations and the breath of life animated them. Maa Ngala Ba had generated a whole world and was glad to see it live.

Then one day, Maa Ngala Ba had a new idea.
She took a bit of what she had already created,
made a mixture and created a dozen people.

She said, "I created the sun and other stars,
And I asked them to shine, to shine through
the eras.

I created the wind,
And I asked it to blow, blow through the universe.

I created the earth,
And I asked it to turn,
turn day and night.

8

I created the rain,
And I asked it to fall, fall and wet the earth.

And now I have
created you, humans
beings, from the wind,
light, earth and water.

I created you with a will.
I gave you freedom.
I gave you creativity.
I will give you part of my name.
I will call you Maa."

These were the first free human beings, free even from Maa Ngala Ba who created them. At first the Maa had an easy life, a life of love, a harmonious life, spending much of their time resting, having fun and enjoying life.
One day, the Maa decided to multiply, but before they did, they went to talk to Maa Ngala Ba.

They said, "There are so few things that look like us on this great earth. There is water and air everywhere, not to mention light. Animals of the bush occupy more space than us."

"The happiness we have, we would like to share.
The wisdom we acquired, we would like to pass on to human beings like us. You possess the spark of life, help us so we can multiply!"

Maa Ngala Ba replied, "Take a bowl and mix your breath in it. I'll bring the spark of life to the mix and you will watch it. Be attentive at all times."

"Focus all your thoughts on the new lives.
They will use the energy of your breath as food.
Pay attention, because at the slightest distraction,
they will disappear."

So the Maa created a large clay pot and decorated it with geometric figures. They filled it with soil and water. The clay pot was the perfect place to keep their mixed breath and they named it *Muu*.

The Maa mixed their breath, and Maa Ngala Ba brought the spark of life to it. The Maa did their best to watch the new lives.

They devoted their thoughts
and the energy of their
breath, and fed them at
every moment, taking turns.

But the new lives did not survive, despite their care.
A brief moment of inattention was enough for them to
disappear. They would fly away into the wind and join
the stars, or they would sink underground.
Sometimes, they would even follow the stream of rivers
to the great sea.

"What are we going to do to keep the new lives born from our mixed breath? We love to move and we cannot always control our thoughts," the Maa asked, complaining to Maa Ngala Ba. "We cannot remain always alert for the new lives. Help us, Maa Ngala Ba!"

Maa Ngala Ba replied,
"I don't want to create
anything for you.
I gave you the power
to create."

Then the Maa had an idea,
"Maa Ngala Ba,
if you don't want to
create anything around
us, at least you can create
something in us. It is you
who made us human
beings. Help us to keep
the breath mixed in our
stomachs," they proposed.

"That way, we can feed them with our blood and we can breathe for them, because we won't forget to breathe for ourselves. We won't need to watch the clay pot because it will be in us."

Maa Ngala Ba said,
"I'll help you. I will place
the clay pot in your bellies.
You can keep your mixed
breath in it. But I will need
volunteers." The Maa who
volunteered were called
Muu-So, those who carry
the *Muu*.

Maa Ngala Ba said,
"To those who are willing
to carry the Muu, I will give
the power of balance and
a sense of justice.
They will come back to life
again and again in future
generations to give birth to
real new lives, new minds
and new worlds."

And so it is.

Coumba Toure

Coumba Toure comes from Mali and Senegal, in West Africa. With Muu-So, she has crafted a tale of the beauty of the process of creation and how it is also necessary to closely care for and love that which we are responsible for.

Rokhaya Gueye

Ndeye Rokhaya Gueye is a visual arts teacher. She completed her studies at the national School of Art in Senegal in 2001 and has since participated, lead and collaborated in multiple art projects. She is also a member of the Art Critique Association in Senegal. This is her first children's book.

Made in the USA
Monee, IL
07 July 2026